Holding on to Your Children

Maintaining a Strong Bond with Your Children in the Face of Societal Influences (Parental Influence Over Peer Influence)

By

Lisa B. Bennett

Disclaimer

The content within this book serves solely for general informational purposes. The author, publisher, and contributors make no explicit or implied representations or warranties regarding the completeness, accuracy, reliability, suitability, or availability of the content. Any reliance on this information is at your own risk.

The author's views and opinions expressed herein are personal and may not align with the official policy or stance of any mentioned organization or individual. The author and publisher disclaim liability for errors or omissions in the information, as well as any losses, injuries, or damages resulting from its utilization.

This book does not intend to offer legal or professional advice. Readers are encouraged to consult appropriate professionals for advice tailored to their specific situations. The author and publisher deny responsibility for any adverse effects or consequences stemming from the information's use.

Including links to external websites or resources does not indicate endorsement or validation of their content. The author and publisher are not accountable for the external content or resource availability.

By reading this book, the reader acknowledges and agrees to the terms outlined in this disclaimer.

About the Author

Lisa B. Bennet is a seasoned writer deeply passionate about fostering human connections, particularly within the realm of parent-child relationships. With a sincere commitment to exploring and enhancing the bonds between parents and their children, Lisa's work revolves around the intricate dynamics of parenting and relationships.

Her body of work spans insightful books dedicated to parenting and relationships, where she shares valuable perspectives on navigating the complexities of raising the next generation. Lisa brings a compassionate touch to the evolving journey of parenthood, offering practical insights and heartfelt advice to readers seeking a deeper understanding of family connections.

Driven by a genuine concern for human connection, Lisa emphasizes the importance of empathy, respect, and meaningful bonds in her exploration of parenting and relationship dynamics. Her writing resonates with diverse audiences, encouraging introspection and fostering a profound appreciation for the ties that bind us as individuals and as a society.

Through her literary contributions, Lisa B. Bennet aims to inspire and guide readers on a journey towards establishing strong and enduring connections within the intricate tapestry of family and relationships.

Table of contents

Introduction

In today's chaotic world, where the influence of friends and peers appears more pronounced than ever, navigating parenthood can feel like maneuvering through a maze. This is the essence of "Holding On to Your Children" – an exploration into the challenges of parenting in an environment where external influences constantly surround our kids.

As we embark on this journey, we confront the reality that peer relationships often wield a powerful and sometimes overwhelming influence in our children's lives. The central question emerges: "How do we distinguish ourselves as parents when the influence of friends is so significant?" It's a genuine struggle, and this journey is a quest to determine how we can make our impact truly matter.

This book goes beyond traditional parent-child relationships, tackling a fundamental question: What is the role of a parent in a world filled with friends, screens, and virtual connections? The solution lies in understanding that, amidst the clamor of this world, parental influence isn't waning – it's transforming into a new and different shape.m.

In an era where everyone seems more connected yet, at times, more distant, "Holding On to Your Children" narrates a story of the enduring strength of parental guidance. It serves as a reminder that, as parents, we aren't losing relevance; we are adapting. It is a call to unite and affirm, "Our influence matters, and it is crucial in guiding our kids through their challenges."

In these chapters, we'll delve into the complexities of attachment, counter-will, and the dangers of emotional distance. Each section offers an opportunity to strengthen the ties that bind us to our children. The emphasis is not on exerting control but on fostering a genuine connection. This process entails constructing trust that resonates more powerfully than the external influences pulling our kids in different directions.

So, as we embark on this journey, let's bear in mind that being a parent isn't solely about authority; it's about establishing a genuine connection. "Holding On to Your Children" is a commitment to rediscover, redefine, and reinforce the essence of parenting in a world where influence is undergoing a shift. Because, ultimately, parents matter more than ever.

Chapter 1

Twisted Bonds, Modified Instincts

Effect of Twisted Attachment Dynamics on Parent-Child Relationships

When the bonds between parents and children become entangled, it resembles a storm swirling through the core of the family. We've all experienced it—the silent connection that is expected to be present, but at times, it becomes disoriented. Picture trying to converse with your child, yet it feels like you're speaking different languages. This complexity arises when attachment, the unseen emotional thread, becomes disrupted. Trust, the usual adhesive holding everything together, takes a blow. It's akin to questioning whether the ground beneath you is as stable as it once was. Both parents and children may feel somewhat adrift, unsure if they can rely on each other as they once did.

Next comes an emotional disconnection that gradually infiltrates. In a well-functioning relationship, emotions naturally circulate, but in the case of a distorted attachment, it's akin to encountering an impediment, like a dam blocking the way. Parents may struggle to grasp their child's emotions, and children may find it difficult to articulate their feelings. This results in an emotional void that can foster a sense of distance, even when individuals are physically present in the same room.

Now, let's delve into behavior—it can become a rollercoaster. When there are issues in the attachment department, children might display acting out, withdrawal, or perhaps seek attention in less-than-ideal ways. It's their way of coping with the uncertainty stemming from an unstable emotional foundation. The noteworthy aspect is that the impact doesn't dissipate with time; it lingers, shaping how we navigate relationships as adults. Identifying these patterns early on is akin to saying, "Let's rewrite the script for the better."

Grasping the consequences of a disturbed attachment is like bringing light into a shadowed room. It marks the first step in addressing the issue, requiring self-reflection, transparent communication, and the creation of a secure emotional environment to rebuild trust and revive the genuine connection we all desire. This undertaking encompasses healing, resilience, and a dedication to reshaping the narrative for more wholesome relationship dynamics in the future.

Envision this as a journey—a voyage to unravel knots, iron out bumps, and rediscover the robust, unbreakable bonds that should exist between parents and children. It refrains from assigning blame and instead centers on understanding that life can be messy, yet it is never too late to embark on the path of rectification.

During this journey, it's crucial to take a moment to assess and recognize the indicators. Are conversations tense? Is trust faltering? Maybe there's an expanding emotional gap. Acknowledging these elements is vital; as humans, we all face challenges, and openly addressing them becomes a collective commitment. It's comparable to acknowledging, "We need to unravel some complexities, but we're in this together."

As parents juggle myriad roles amid the chaos of daily life, the potency of self-reflection becomes apparent. Taking a moment to inquire, "How am I showing up for my child? What patterns am I repeating, and are they constructive?" This isn't about casting blame; it's about cultivating awareness, the kind that paves the way for positive change.

Communication transforms into a refined skill, going beyond simple conversation to embrace genuine listening. It involves establishing an atmosphere where a child truly feels acknowledged, where their thoughts and feelings carry weight. This requires cultivating an environment where both parent and child can openly express themselves without fearing judgment, acknowledging the pivotal role empathy plays in navigating life's intricate dance.

Rebuilding trust mirrors the meticulous repair of a bridge—one brick at a time. Consistency is paramount, exemplified by showing up as promised and being present in those small, meaningful moments. It's about substantiating, through actions, that the connection is steadfast. Importantly, trust is reciprocal; it involves not only children trusting parents but also parents trusting in their capacity to guide and support.

This journey doesn't require flawless execution; instead, it highlights ongoing development. It recognizes that, as parents, we are continuously evolving, and that is entirely acceptable. Each positive stride, irrespective of its scale, signifies a triumph. The aim is to foster a family culture where mistakes are seen as chances to learn, vulnerability is recognized as strength, and love functions as the cohesive force that binds everything together.

Outcomes of Suppressed Parental Instincts

Discussing the consequences of parents stifling their innate instincts is akin to tampering with the core of parenting. Those instinctive feelings that come into play when navigating the challenges of raising a child? Well, when these instincts are set aside or neglected, it creates a ripple effect throughout the entire parent-child relationship.

To begin with, it's akin to navigating without a map. Parental instincts serve as an inherent compass, aiding in decisions about our children. When that compass is suppressed or overshadowed, uncertainty creeps in, leading to hesitations and questioning every parenting decision. It may result in a constant search for advice from others or a sense of guessing, disrupting the organic flow of parenthood.

However, here's the point – children are attuned to these dynamics. They act as emotional detectors, discerning when something is awry. When parents stifle their instincts, children may perceive a gap in the overall picture, disrupting their sense of security and trust in their parents. It's comparable to constructing a robust bridge; if the foundation is unstable, everything else seems somewhat precarious.

Next comes the aspect of behavior. Children are akin to sponges, absorbing everything in their surroundings. When parents deviate from their instincts, it creates a void in establishing clear boundaries and guidance. Children may resort to acting out or seeking attention in less-than-ideal ways. It's as if they are attempting to compensate for the gaps left by the suppressed instincts, resulting in a challenging journey in parenting.

Moreover, it's not a transient situation; it leaves a lasting imprint. If children witness their parents frequently doubting themselves, it can affect the children's capacity to trust their own instincts in the future. They might experience uncertainty when making decisions or lack confidence in their judgment. It's akin to transmitting a legacy of self-doubt.

But here's the positive aspect – acknowledging this suppression is the initial stride toward rectifying it. It involves pausing to contemplate your own parenting, comprehending the origins of those doubts and hesitations. Parenting isn't about adhering strictly to a rulebook; instead, it's about tapping into the instinctive knowledge handed down through generations.

So, it's a voyage, you see? A venture to reestablish a connection with those instinctual feelings, allowing them to lead you in the upbringing of your children. It involves affirming, "Hey, my instincts hold significance, and they're worth heeding." Because, ultimately, parenting is a complex dance, a rhythm derived from trusting your instincts and establishing an environment where your kids can experience security and connection. It's about unraveling the knots, ironing out the bumps, and rediscovering the inherent, instinctive flow of parenthood.

Chapter 2

The Causes of the Breakdown

Societal Factors Contributing to the Breakdown of Traditional Parenting Structures

Have you observed the shift in parenting nowadays? It feels like we're navigating an entirely new landscape, and it's undeniable—things have evolved. Technology plays a significant role in this change, with the digital age introducing exciting advancements while altering the traditional aspects of children's upbringing. Screens, social media, and a constant influx of information are now integral, reshaping the once-familiar elements of face-to-face interactions, outdoor play, and limited exposure to external influences, making them seem like relics of the past.

Discussing influences, social media has transformed the landscape. It goes beyond mere connections among friends; it's a realm where kids actively seek recognition and validation. Parents now contend with a virtual world that sometimes carries more weight than their own voices, creating a challenge in shaping their children's beliefs and behaviors. The family dynamic has also shifted. Traditional nuclear families, with defined gender roles and two parents, now share the stage with diverse setups like single-parent households, same-sex parents, and blended families. While diversity is positive, it introduces complexity for parents. Extended family networks, once supportive, are occasionally replaced by more isolated structures. Grandparents, aunts, and uncles, once crucial to childcare, are often farther away, leaving parents to navigate the journey with fewer resources and an increased need for self-reliance.

Finances play a significant role. Coping with the challenge of meeting financial demands in a world that constantly requires more can be daunting. While having dual incomes may boost the bank account, it can also strain parents, reducing the time and energy available for essential matters, such as being present for their children. The pursuit of career success and material wealth may overshadow parenting, upsetting the delicate equilibrium between earning a living and raising a child.

Education becomes a factor influencing the dynamics between parents and children. The contemporary education system extends beyond mere learning; it encompasses various aspects. Parents often immerse themselves in tasks like homework and extracurricular activities, losing the traditional approach of letting kids discover their own paths. The emphasis on academic success may create stress, potentially putting a strain on the parent-child relationship.

Societal expectations and cultural changes also come into play. The conventional ideals of normalcy or success may conflict with traditional parenting beliefs. Challenges arise from factors like gender roles, individualism, and the pursuit of achievement, making it difficult for parents to strike a balance between offering guidance and allowing their children the freedom to carve out their own paths.

Globalization is a key player. In a world where cultures blend, and individuals are exposed to diverse influences, traditional practices can seem outdated in this global mosaic. Parents must navigate a more fluid landscape, embracing new perspectives and being open to adapting to change.

Chapter 3

The Influence of Parents is Diminishing

The Slow Erosion of Parental Power and Impact

This mirrors an intricate interconnection of changes in society, cultural shifts, and evolving dynamics within families. It's like observing the gradual erosion of a once-sturdy foundation, influenced by various factors.

A significant element is the growing impact of external influences like media and peers. In the digital era, children encounter a wide range of information and perspectives beyond their family sphere. Social media, in particular, serves as a potent influencer, molding opinions and values that may occasionally differ from parental teachings. It's akin to a continuous flow of external voices, contributing to the slow attenuation of parental influence.

The evolving structure of family units contributes to this shift. The traditional hierarchical authority in families has transitioned to more egalitarian models. While promoting equality is beneficial, it can occasionally lead to a blurred distinction in traditional parental authority. It resembles a recalibration of power dynamics, redefining the central role of parents within the evolving concept of family.

Economic factors play a crucial role in diminishing parental influence. In households where both parents have jobs outside the home, time becomes scarce. Balancing work obligations and parenting responsibilities can reduce the quantity and quality of time parents dedicate to their children. This time constraint opens the door for other influences like schools, media, and peers to play a role in shaping the child's perspective. It's akin to a gradual change in the balance of who significantly impacts a child's development.

The educational system contributes to this diminishing influence. As schools assume a more central role in children's lives, parents may discover that educational institutions exert a substantial influence on their child's values and beliefs. The impact of teachers, classmates, and the overall school environment can at times overshadow the guidance offered by parents. It's comparable to the educational sphere evolving into a parallel authority structure, contributing to the gradual erosion of parental influence.

Furthermore, societal views on authority have changed. The focus on individual autonomy and personal agency occasionally conflicts with conventional models of parental authority. Children are urged to express themselves, challenge authority, and make decisions from a young age. While promoting independence is essential, it can contribute to the gradual reduction of the unquestioned influence parents previously maintained.

Instances where Attachment Dynamics may Unintentionally hinder Effective Parenting

Let's delve into scenarios where attachment dynamics, usually a foundation of emotional connection, can inadvertently impede successful parenting. It's akin to uncovering layers to comprehend how something fundamentally positive can at times present difficulties in the parenting domain.

An example is when attachment becomes imbalanced, resulting in an excessively reliant relationship. While attachment promotes emotional security, an overly dependent connection with a parent can hinder a child's development of autonomy and self-reliance. It's akin to maintaining a delicate equilibrium—nurturing attachment without inadvertently suppressing a child's capability to independently navigate the world.

Another difficulty emerges when attachment dynamics become excessively intertwined, blurring the lines between parent and child. In these instances, the parent's emotions, objectives, or needs become interwoven with those of the child. This enmeshment can impede the child's development of an individual identity and hinder their ability to establish healthy boundaries. It's comparable to a merging of emotional spaces, where the distinct emotional territories of parent and child overlap, potentially obstructing the child's progression toward independence.

Counter-will, a phenomenon where a child opposes external influence, can also be associated with attachment dynamics. While a child's autonomy is crucial, continual counter-will can disrupt effective parenting. Attachment dynamics, if excessively restrictive or authoritarian, might inadvertently fuel a child's resistance. It's akin to a tug-of-war dynamic, where the child's wish for independence clashes with a type of attachment that unintentionally constrains their autonomy. Furthermore, attachment dynamics might inadvertently play a role in emotional patterns, such as emotional co-dependency. If a child consistently depends on a parent for emotional regulation without developing their coping mechanisms, it can result in difficulties in managing emotions independently. This unintended entanglement can impede the child's emotional resilience. It resembles a pattern where the child heavily relies on the parent as a consistent emotional support, potentially constraining their ability to navigate emotional challenges autonomously.

Attachment dynamics may also unintentionally foster a sense of learned helplessness. If a parent consistently steps in to resolve every challenge the child encounters, it might inadvertently convey that the child is incapable of handling difficulties independently. This learned helplessness can impede the development of problem-solving skills and resilience. It's akin to inadvertently sending a message that the child lacks the ability to overcome obstacles autonomously.

Counter-will Influence on the Development of Defiant Behavior in Children

Let's explore the concept of counter-will and its manifestation in children's disobedient behavior. It's akin to comprehending the reasons behind their occasional resistance to our instructions.

Counter-will is essentially their expression of, "Wait, I want to do things my way." It's not necessarily defiance; it's more about asserting their independence. Imagine a young child confidently saying "no" when you're encouraging them to eat their vegetables or tidy up – that's counter-will in practice.

In childhood, it's completely typical. Children are discovering their individuality and preferences. The phase of asserting "I can do it myself"? That's also counter-will in play, and it's a healthy aspect of the maturation process.

However, here's the catch – if we, as parents, consistently react to this resistance with strict discipline, it can escalate into outright disobedience. The continual push against their autonomy might lead them to believe they need to rebel to retain some control over their own choices. It's a response to feeling restricted, and disobedience becomes their method of asserting, "I'm in charge here."

At times, their internal conflicts intensify the counter-will. They might sincerely wish to comply with our requests but also sense a need to resist for no particular reason. This internal struggle can result in disobedient behavior, as if they're attempting to reconcile their willingness to cooperate with their inherent resistance.

The crucial aspect is our response. Providing choices and alternatives can make a significant difference. It's akin to allowing them a voice in the situation, enabling them to feel a sense of control within defined boundaries. When they have options, it shifts the focus from resistance to decision-making. It's about guiding them towards cooperation by recognizing their preferences and granting them some influence. Understanding counter-will requires recognizing it as a natural facet of a child's development. It's not about suppressing their independence but rather about navigating this phase in a constructive manner. By offering choices and respecting their need for a sense of control, we can redirect potential disobedience into a cooperative interaction. This approach not only fosters a positive trajectory in the parent-child relationship but also encourages the child's autonomy and decision-making skills. Acknowledging and effectively managing counter-will becomes a crucial step in nurturing a healthy and supportive environment for the child's overall development.

Chapter 4

Parent-Child Bond and The Peer

How Peer Influence Can Disturb the Connection Between Parents and Children

Sure, let's discuss how friends can occasionally impact the parent-child dynamic. Picture it as a dance – as a parent, you have your steps and rhythm, and then these friends come in, adding their own moves that don't quite align.

Certainly, friends introduce a whole new set of perspectives and behaviors. It becomes a continuous juggling act between the lessons you aim to impart at home and the trends your child adopts from their peers. It's navigating the realm of values, and suddenly, there's a conflict between your guidance and the influence of their friends.

It extends beyond ideas; it's also about communication. The language, the attitudes – everything can shift when they're with friends. It's as if there's an entirely different code that doesn't quite align with the home environment. Communication becomes a balancing act between the familiar language and the one your child adopts from their friends.

As your child matures, the significance of friends increases. The desire for independence arises, and it seems like parents are in a competition with friends for influence. Friends begin to take the lead, creating a sense that the parent-child bond is now facing an external force that is suddenly taking control.

Then there's the subtlety of peer pressure. Friends can exert a significant influence on decisions, from clothing choices to activities. When the pressure to conform intensifies, it can strongly contradict the values parents aim to instill. It's as if parents are maneuvering through this delicate terrain where their aspirations for their child clash with the expectations set by friends.

Emotionally, friends also wield significant influence. The strong desire to belong and be accepted is particularly pronounced in the teenage years. If aligning with friends' expectations brings more social acceptance, it could take precedence over the emotional connection with parents. Suddenly, the emotional closeness parents aspire to takes a secondary position to the immediate validation offered by friends.

It's not solely about behaviors; it can impact how kids perceive authority. In their quest for greater independence, friends might become influential figures challenging or questioning parental authority. It's as if parents are caught in a power struggle with friends who hold a different kind of influence.

In the digital era, the impact of friends goes beyond in-person interactions. Social media intensifies this influence, establishing a virtual space where friends' opinions and trends carry significant weight. Parents grapple with this additional layer, where influence stems not only from real-life interactions but also from screens.

Reclaiming and Reconnecting With Our Children After a Peer Influence

Reconnecting with our children after their friends' influence is like strengthening a bridge that might have become shaky. The goal is not merely to revert to the past but to build something more robust.

First and foremost, reclaiming that connection involves conveying, "I'm still here for you." Peer influence can create a peculiar distance, where friends suddenly seem more important. Reclaiming means demonstrating to your child that your support is unwavering, regardless of external influences. It's about restoring the closeness that lies at the core of being a parent.

Reconnecting is like finding a new rhythm together. Friends introduce a different atmosphere, a distinct way of speaking and behaving that may not align with what you're accustomed to. Reconnecting is about adapting to these changes, embracing flexibility, and discovering common ground. It's akin to adjusting your dance steps to sync with the new rhythm your child picked up from their friends.

Next is the element of values. Occasionally, friends may steer children towards choices conflicting with your teachings. Through active involvement, you're strengthening familial principles that transcend external pressures, essentially stating, "This defines us, and I'm here to redirect you if you stray."

Listening plays a significant role in this process. Reclaiming involves creating a space where your child feels comfortable talking to you. It's akin to providing a safe haven where they can share their thoughts without fearing judgment. Ensuring they feel heard and understood is pivotal in rebuilding that connection.

Reconnecting isn't a one-way street; it's a collaborative effort. Encouraging open conversations, showing empathy, and ensuring your child feels like a part of the rebuilding process are all crucial. It's like both of you working together to construct a bridge that connects your worlds. Acknowledging what they've experienced while reinforcing the strong bond between you.

What's fascinating is that it's not about eliminating the influence friends bring. Instead, reclaiming and reconnecting mean deriving lessons from those encounters. It's akin to turning a difficulty into a chance for parents and kids to evolve together. It becomes a mutual journey, enhancing understanding and fortifying the bond.

Guidance on Fostering Strong, Empowering Connections With Our Children

Cultivating strong, empowering relationships with our children is akin to tending a garden – it demands time, attention, and abundant care.

First and foremost, prioritize communication. Establish an open, non-judgmental space where your child feels at ease expressing their thoughts and emotions. Practice active listening without immediately jumping into advice mode, recognizing that sometimes they simply need someone to listen. Immerse yourself in their lives. Participate in shared activities, whether playing games, cooking, or engaging in conversation. Quality time reinforces the bond, signaling that you value and enjoy their company. Seek to understand their world. Take an interest in their hobbies, passions, and concerns. This not only demonstrates care but also facilitates a deeper connection. Knowing what matters to them helps build a bridge of understanding. Foster empowerment through decision-making. Engage them in choices suitable for their age, providing a sense of autonomy and expressing that their opinions are meaningful. This conveys trust in their decision-making abilities and assures them of your support. Set clear, consistent boundaries. Boundaries offer security and help children grasp expectations. Find the right balance between freedom and guidance toward responsible choices. Demonstrate positive conduct. Children absorb lessons through observation. Display the values and behaviors you aim to cultivate, reinforcing the principles you want them to embrace, be it kindness, resilience, or empathy. Celebrate their strengths.

Acknowledge and rejoice in their accomplishments, no matter how small. Focusing on strengths builds confidence and fosters a positive self-image, akin to saying, "You're doing great!".

Instill problem-solving skills and resilience. Life presents challenges, and guiding them through solving problems underscores that setbacks are chances for learning and personal development. Acknowledge and validate their emotions. Emotions are intricate; let them know it's okay to feel a spectrum of emotions. Validating their feelings nurtures emotional intelligence and bolsters the connection.

Express love and affection regularly. Articulate your love, embrace them, and show physical affection. These small gestures create a nurturing environment, reinforcing the emotional bond between parent and child.

Finally, exercise patience. Developing a strong, empowering connection is a gradual journey demanding consistency, understanding, and adaptability. Similar to nurturing a garden, witness its gradual growth and flourishing, understanding that the invested effort contributes to a resilient and profoundly connected relationship with your child.

Chapter 5

The Stagnation of Cultural Progress

The Impact of Cultural Shifts on The Parent-Child Connection

Examining how cultural shifts affect the parent-child connection unveils a complex interplay of societal changes that resonate within family dynamics. It entails deciphering the subtle influences that mold the evolving relationship between parents and their children.

A significant impact emerges from the changing dynamics of family structures. Cultural shifts often reconfigure traditional roles within households. As expectations related to gender, work, and societal norms undergo changes, the interplay between parents and children undergoes a nuanced yet profound adjustment. It's comparable to recalibrating the family compass, shaping how parents engage with and understand their children in this evolving cultural landscape.

The ascent of technology and social media adds another layer to the parent-child connection. In the digital age, communication transcends face-to-face interactions, extending into the realm of screens and online platforms. This shift not only alters the modes of communication but also the nature of the interactions. It's akin to navigating a dual reality where the rules of engagement differ, affecting the depth and texture of the parent-child bond.

Cultural changes influence parenting methods. Shifting societal values impact how parents navigate raising their children. Fresh outlooks on independence, discipline, and emotional expression shape the approaches parents take. It's akin to a continuous conversation between the past and the present, where evolving cultural norms provide a context for the unfolding parent-child connection.

The accelerated pace of modern life exacerbates the impact of cultural shifts. Hectic schedules, demanding work environments, and a constant influx of information create a fast-paced lifestyle. This can pose challenges to the amount of time and undivided attention parents can dedicate to their children. It's reminiscent of a time-strapped reality, where the rush of daily life can occasionally act as a barrier to deepening the parent-child relationship.

Cultural variety brings an additional layer. In a globally connected world, families frequently weave through a fabric of cultural influences. While this diversity enhances the parent-child connection by exposing children to diverse perspectives, it also poses challenges in harmonizing cultural distinctions. It's akin to conducting a symphony of experiences, where the seamless integration of diverse elements adds to the depth and intricacy of the parent-child relationship.

The Challenges posed by a Culture Dominated by Peer Relationships

Navigating a culture where peer relationships take precedence presents unique challenges that can have a substantial impact on individuals, especially in their formative years. It's comparable to maneuvering through a maze where the viewpoints and anticipations of peers play a pivotal role.

A notable difficulty arises from the pressure to conform. In a culture centered around peers, the primary focus is on assimilating. The urge for acceptance and validation from peers can result in individuals compromising their values, preferences, or genuine selves. It's comparable to navigating a delicate balance between staying true to oneself and following the unspoken norms of the peer group.

Furthermore, peer influence can sometimes overshadow guidance from family and other support systems. Traditional sources of wisdom, such as parents or mentors, may contend with the immediacy and intensity of peer opinions. This shift in influence balance, where external validation from peers becomes a driving force, has the potential to dilute the impact of familial guidance. The overwhelming influence of peer relationships may instill a fear of being excluded. Dynamics within peer groups frequently encompass the anxiety of being left out or isolated, influencing behavior and decision-making. This fear can lead individuals to prioritize peer approval over their well-being or values, creating a persistent undercurrent of anxiety that affects choices to uphold social inclusion. In a culture where peer relationships prevail, there's a risk of losing individual identity. The emphasis on group dynamics may overshadow the importance of personal growth and self-discovery, leading to a collective identity where individual traits and aspirations take a back seat to shared values and norms of the peer group. The widespread use of social media exacerbates these challenges, transforming online platforms into a forum for peer interactions. This increases the pressure to carefully craft a particular image or adhere to trends, resembling living in a digital fishbowl where continuous peer scrutiny fosters feelings of inadequacy or the constant need for validation. Additionally, the dominance of peer relationships can impact mental health, contributing to stress, anxiety, and issues like low self-esteem. It's akin to carrying a mental load shaped by peer dynamics, affecting overall well-being. Grasping these challenges is essential for individuals navigating a culture where peer relationships hold sway. It requires cultivating a robust self-awareness, resilience against peer pressure, and the skill to strike a balance between the significance of peer connections and individual values and well-being. It's akin to navigating a complex maze, recognizing peer influences while preserving an authentic sense of identity.

The consequences of Avoiding Emotional Engagement in Parenting

Overlooking the emotional connection in parenting has substantial consequences. It's similar to neglecting the essence of the parent-child relationship, and this absence can create a lasting impact on a child's development.

A significant outcome is the risk of lacking emotional support. Children need recognition of their emotions, validation of their experiences, and a stable emotional base to depend on. If parents neglect this emotional connection, it's akin to abandoning a child to navigate the complex emotions alone, potentially leading to challenges in managing their feelings.

Another issue is attachment. Emotional engagement acts as the adhesive forming a secure bond between a parent and a child. If parents refrain from getting emotionally involved, it can result in an insecure attachment. Imagine it as omitting a key ingredient in the recipe for how a child learns to trust and connect with others.

Communication is adversely affected as well. Emotional engagement involves actively listening, demonstrating empathy, and understanding. When these elements are absent, it's comparable to trying to build a bridge without the essential tools, resulting in strained communication where the child feels ignored or disregarded.

The impact extends into a child's social and emotional growth. Emotional engagement plays a crucial role in developing social skills and emotional intelligence. In its absence, children might struggle in social situations, have difficulty understanding their own emotions, and find it challenging to connect with others. It's like skipping a vital step in their emotional and social learning journey.

Moreover, there are behavioral challenges. Children might act out or seek attention if their emotional needs aren't met. It's as if they're sending signals in a language parents might find challenging to decipher, resulting in behaviors that can be difficult to manage.

Chapter 6

Caught in The Grip of Immaturity

The Challenges Associated With Children stuck in Emotional and Behavioral Immaturity

Dealing with the difficulties linked to children encountering emotional and behavioral immaturity is like maneuvering through a maze where understanding and patience serve as the guiding principles. This undertaking includes addressing the elements contributing to this stagnation and steering children toward emotional development.

A challenge lies in recognizing indications of emotional and behavioral immaturity, resembling the complexity of unraveling a puzzle where specific behaviors may signal a requirement for additional support. Essential to this process is acknowledging the underlying causes, as emotional and behavioral immaturity can stem from elements such as unresolved emotional problems, trauma, or environmental stressors. Identifying these root causes is the primary step toward implementing effective intervention.

Establishing consistent and clear boundaries is pivotal. Similar to creating a safety net, providing a framework helps children understand expectations and consequences, enabling them to explore and express themselves responsibly. Encouraging age-appropriate independence is another key aspect, akin to providing stepping stones toward autonomy and allowing choices within safe limits.

Emphasizing emotional intelligence is vital, providing children with skills to effectively identify and regulate emotions. This strategy encourages mature emotional responses, playing a role in their emotional and behavioral growth. Establishing a supportive environment is equally important, similar to building a nurturing space where children feel free to express themselves without the fear of judgment, fostering a positive emotional exchange.

Seeking professional assistance when needed is not indicative of failure but a proactive measure for support. Consulting specialists in emotional and behavioral challenges is akin to seeking guidance from a maze navigator, assisting in navigating the intricacies of a child's emotional terrain. Maintaining consistent communication among parents, caregivers, and educators is crucial, constructing a bridge that ensures everyone is aligned regarding a child's emotional and behavioral development. Sharing insights and observations promotes a collaborative approach to addressing and overcoming challenges.

The Role of Parenting in the Development of Aggressive or Victimized Behavior

Examining how parenting influences the development of aggressive or victimized behavior in children unveils a complex interplay of factors shaping their social and emotional environment. It's comparable to unraveling the threads that contribute to the dynamics of aggression and victimization within the realm of parenting.

Firstly, the chosen parenting style holds a pivotal role. Authoritarian or excessively permissive approaches can contribute to the development of aggressive behavior. Authoritarian styles, characterized by strict rules and punishment, may trigger defiance or aggression. Conversely, permissive styles, lacking clear boundaries, might result in a deficiency of impulse control and empathy. Achieving a delicate balance, setting boundaries without being overly restrictive, fosters a sense of discipline and empathy in the child.

The quality of the parent-child relationship is paramount. A warm and supportive relationship serves as a buffer against aggressive tendencies. Secure and loved children are less likely to resort to aggressive behaviors. Conversely, a lack of emotional connection or inconsistent support can contribute to the development of aggression or victimization. It's like the emotional foundation that either shields or exposes children to the risk of aggressive behavior.

Demonstrating behavior has a significant impact. Children observe and absorb their parents' actions and responses. When parents display or support aggressive behavior in handling conflicts, children tend to imitate these patterns. In contrast, parents who exemplify healthy communication and conflict resolution contribute to fostering a more positive social environment. It's akin to a mirror reflecting either constructive or destructive behaviors.

Parental involvement in monitoring and guiding a child's social interactions is crucial. Parents actively teaching empathy, perspective-taking, and problem-solving help prevent aggressive or victimized behavior. Insufficient supervision or guidance can leave children susceptible to negative peer influences. It's like providing a compass to help children navigate the complexities of social dynamics.

Maintaining consistent approaches to discipline is crucial. When consequences for aggressive behavior vary inconsistently, it can confuse children and hinder the development of self-control. Clear and consistent consequences, along with positive reinforcement for prosocial behaviors, play a role in shaping appropriate social conduct. This process is akin to setting up a roadmap to assist children in comprehending the consequences of their actions.

Addressing and intervening promptly in aggressive behavior is vital. Parental responsiveness to signs of aggression or victimization demonstrates a commitment to fostering a healthy social environment. It's like identifying potential issues early on, addressing them, and providing necessary support to prevent further escalation.

The Complexities of Addressing Sexuality in The Context of Parent-child Relationships

Addressing sexuality within parent-child relationships is comparable to embarking on a delicate journey where communication, respect, and understanding act as guiding principles. This involves acknowledging the sensitivity of the topic and establishing an environment that fosters open dialogue while respecting the individual boundaries of both parents and children. Initiating conversations about sexuality requires timing and tact. Finding natural opportunities, such as during relevant discussions or moments portrayed in media, creates a comfortable entry point. It's akin to choosing a path aligned with the flow of daily life, making the conversation feel less forced and more organic.

Creating a safe space for open communication is crucial. Establishing trust is like laying a foundation where children feel at ease discussing sensitive topics without fear of judgment. Encouraging questions and actively listening without imposing personal biases contribute to this environment of trust. Valuing individual comfort levels is of utmost importance. Children might respond differently and pose varying questions influenced by their unique personalities and experiences. Acknowledging and respecting these differences is comparable to navigating varied terrains, adjusting the approach to cater to each child's needs and understanding.

Providing accurate and age-appropriate information is essential. Tailoring discussions to a child's developmental stage ensures that the information is relevant and understandable. It's like offering a map that aligns with the child's current level of comprehension, gradually introducing more complex details as they mature. Employing inclusive language and steering clear of stigmatization is crucial. Discussing sexuality without attaching shame or judgment aids children in cultivating a healthy and positive attitude towards their bodies and relationships. It's akin to removing obstacles that could impede a child's understanding or acceptance of diverse expressions of sexuality.

Encouraging a two-way dialogue is vital. While parents provide information, creating an environment where children feel comfortable expressing their thoughts and asking questions fosters mutual understanding. It's like a conversation where both parties contribute to the exploration of this complex and personal aspect of life. Recognizing the importance of privacy becomes crucial, particularly as children reach adolescence. Striking a balance between openness and acknowledging their need for personal space is akin to delicately navigating a dance. This ensures that children feel they can trust their parents while cultivating a sense of autonomy in their exploration of sexuality.

Addressing values and cultural beliefs surrounding sexuality is also part of the journey. Parents may share their perspectives while acknowledging that children may form their own beliefs as they grow. It's like providing a compass that aligns with family values while recognizing the importance of individual exploration and understanding.

The Manifestation of Aggression in Children and its Legal Implications

Examining how aggression manifests in children entails a nuanced investigation where comprehending behavioral dynamics intersects with the intricacies of legal consequences. It's like unraveling layers to identify the origins of aggression while taking into account the legal context surrounding such behavior in children.

Children's aggression can manifest diversely, encompassing physical, verbal, or relational expressions. Physical aggression involves harmful acts, such as hitting or pushing. Verbal aggression includes threats, insults, or hostile language, while relational aggression comprises social manipulation or exclusion. Identifying these manifestations is akin to decoding a language that communicates unmet needs or emotional struggles.

Understanding the causes of aggression is crucial, as it may stem from factors like unmet emotional needs, exposure to violence, inconsistent discipline, or underlying mental health issues. It's akin to untangling a web of influences contributing to aggressive behavior expression, requiring a holistic approach to address the root causes.

Legal ramifications arise when aggression leads to harm to others or property. Depending on severity and circumstances, consequences within the legal system may vary from warnings and counseling to engagement with the juvenile justice system. Maneuvering through this legal terrain is akin to walking a tightrope, maintaining a balance between holding the child accountable and acknowledging their developmental stage and potential for change.

Early intervention is vital to prevent escalation. Recognizing signs of aggression and addressing underlying issues through counseling or therapeutic interventions is like applying a preemptive strategy to redirect the trajectory of a child's behavior. Early intervention can mitigate legal consequences and contribute to more positive outcomes.

The significance of parents and caregivers cannot be overstated. Setting clear expectations, maintaining consistent discipline, and fostering a supportive environment act as constructing a protective shield against the emergence of aggression. Parents also have a vital responsibility in seeking professional assistance if necessary, ensuring a holistic approach to addressing underlying issues.

Legal consequences may vary based on jurisdiction and the age of the child. Some legal systems prioritize rehabilitation over punitive measures for juvenile offenders, recognizing the potential for growth and change. It's like navigating a legal landscape that aims to strike a balance between accountability and the developmental stage of the child.

Educational institutions also play a role in addressing aggression. Implementing anti-bullying programs, fostering a positive school climate, and providing counseling services contribute to a supportive environment that discourages aggressive behavior. It's like creating a foundation within the educational system that promotes empathy, conflict resolution, and positive social interactions.

Chapter 7

Recreate the Attachment Village

Community Support in Nurturing Healthy Parent-child Relationships

Let's discuss why community support serves as the foundation for robust parent-child relationships. Parenting is an adventurous journey, and the good news is, you don't have to go through it alone. Connecting with fellow parents is like finding a tribe that understands the challenges. Sharing stories, exchanging advice – suddenly, you realize you're not alone in the rollercoaster of parenting.

Communities provide a wealth of resources, from parenting classes to support groups, acting as a toolbox filled with valuable resources. It's not just about surviving; it's about thriving as a parent with the right tools and knowledge at your fingertips.

Having emotional support is vital during challenging times, and community backing serves as a safety net, prepared to catch you when faced with difficulties. The presence of a supportive community makes navigating tough moments more manageable and reassuring.

It's not only beneficial for parents but also essential for creating a vibrant social world for our kids. Community activities and interactions are like a playground for their social development. They learn to share, communicate, and navigate this big world, all thanks to the supportive community around them. Community support significantly alleviates feelings of isolation and parental stress. If you ever find yourself a bit alone in the parenting journey, a community is akin to an open door, welcoming you for essential social interactions. It serves as a protective shield against isolation, ensuring that everyone experiences a sense of connection and support.

When life throws curveballs, community support steps up its game. It becomes a collective force, offering help and resources when families face unexpected challenges. It's like a safety net on steroids, making sure that no one in the community is left hanging during tough times. Let's celebrate community support as an incredible force that makes the parenting journey easier, more enjoyable, and a whole lot more connected. In the end, it's about recognizing that we're not just raising kids; we're doing it together as a community that cares about each other's well-being.

Holding On to Our Kids in the Era of Technology

Let's address the challenges posed by the prevalence of gadgets in our lives. Living in a screen-dominated world, we encounter moments where technology interferes with quality family time. One approach is designating screen-free moments, like family dinners or specific activities, to reclaim time from digital distractions and prioritize genuine interactions.

Effective communication regarding our technology habits is essential. Setting rules and discussing acceptable screen time collectively is like crafting a shared game plan. Aligning on these aspects reduces stress related to technology use.

Unexpectedly, technology can function as a bonding tool. Participating in activities such as playing video games, enjoying a movie night, or sharing interests online transforms screens into avenues for connection rather than sources of division. Striving for a balance where technology enriches our relationships is the goal. Parents play a pivotal role as tech role models. Children observe and emulate our habits, so modeling a balanced approach to screen time sets a positive example. It involves demonstrating responsible tech use while being fully present in the moment.

Although technology provides convenience, there's no substitute for face-to-face conversations. Choosing real discussions over texting underscores the warmth conveyed through smiles and the subtleties of body language, elements that screens cannot reproduce.

Diversifying our time with creative activities, such as outdoor adventures or DIY projects, contributes to a treasure chest of shared memories. These endeavors offer a respite from screens and foster genuine connections.

Implementing tech-free times is transformative. Whether during dinners or family game nights, these rituals create moments where attention is fully dedicated to each other, reinforcing the significance of authentic connections.

Regular check-ins about our feelings regarding technology usage are essential. Creating a safe space to discuss potential feelings of overwhelm or addiction ensures that we navigate the digital world while staying grounded in what truly matters – our strong family connections.

Conclusion

As we conclude our exploration of "Holding On to Your Kids," it feels akin to reaching the final chapter of a captivating novel – one brimming with insights, challenges, and abundant heart. This isn't merely a collection of words on pages; it has served as a companion, leading us through the twists and turns of modern parenthood.

In a world where screens vie for our attention and parenting confronts new complexities, the essence of this journey lies in grasping why, now more than ever, parents play a crucial role. We've delved into attachment dynamics and traversed the digital age, all with the aim of nurturing resilient connections with our children. Here's to the triumphs – those instances where we gained understanding and deepened connections – and to the trials that educated us, molded us, and transformed us into better parents. "Holding On to Your Children" is more than a book; it has been a dialogue, a contemplation, and a reminder that, amid the chaos, holding onto what truly matters is an act of love, courage, and unwavering commitment.

As we turn the final page, let's carry with us the harmonies of comprehending the impact of distorted attachments, the repercussions of suppressed instincts, and the art of navigating the digital landscape. This isn't a farewell but a celebration – a celebration of family, connection, and the resilience that arises from holding on.

So, here's to the next chapter in your family story – where the dance of parenthood continues, and the echoes of "Holding On to Your Kids" linger as a guiding melody. May your journey be filled with warmth, laughter, and the enduring strength that comes from holding on – not just to the book but to the precious bonds that make your family uniquely yours. Cheers to holding on and embracing the beautiful dance of parenthood that lies ahead.

Leaving a Review

Dear Reader,

I hope this message finds you well. I want to express my sincere gratitude for choosing to explore the contents of this book. The journey has been extraordinary, and I genuinely trust that you found the book both enlightening and valuable.

As an author, your feedback is of great importance to me. I would appreciate it immensely if you could take a moment to share your thoughts and impressions by leaving a review on the platform where you acquired the book.

Your review not only provides valuable insights for me but also serves as a guide for other readers who may be considering whether this book aligns with their needs and interests.

Whether it's a brief comment or a more detailed reflection, your candid feedback is highly cherished.

Thank you once again for being a part of this literary journey. I look forward to hearing your thoughts, and I deeply appreciate the time and consideration you devote to this.

Best regards,

Lisa B. Bennett